Corner Shop COWGIRL

Poems

by

Alison Carr

IRON PRESS

First published 2017 by IRON Press
5 Marden Terrace
Cullercoats
North Shields
NE30 4PD
tel/fax +44(0)191 2531901
ironpress@blueyonder.co.uk
www.ironpress.co.uk

ISBN
Printed by Ingram Lightning Source

Cover and Book Design Brian Grogan

Typeset in Georgia
IRON Press books are distributed by NBNI International
and represented by Inpress Ltd
Churchill House, 12 Mosley Street,
Newcastle upon Tyne, NE1 1DE
tel: +44(0)191 2308104
www.inpressbooks.co.uk

Supported using public funding by
ARTS COUNCIL
ENGLAND
LOTTERY FUNDED

for Wendy and Avril

Contents

Alison Carr

Based in Bishop Auckland, Co. Durham, Alison Carr is one of the North East of England's most prolific poets and has become an accomplished writer exploring ideas around identity with depth and intensity. Alison believes that writing chose her. She is widely published in poetry and prose anthologies, and her first play *Coal Dust Whisper's Song* was published by Mudfog Press in 2010. Alison is widely educated in literature, theatre, art and the classics and she has won literary prizes for her poetry.

Having always enjoyed reading her poetry live, in recent years Alison has turned her attention to the construction of performance pieces with artistic collaborators, using poetry, music, sound, and visuals. Acclaimed productions of her theatre based poetry include *Behind the Masque* (2013), *Matryoshka* (2014) and *Dust of the Street's Shining* (2016).

Alison comments, "I write to survive, my traumatic brain injury as a child impacted on my everyday life in previously unimaginable ways. I am unable to work in the conventional sense other than as a writer and artist, and so I write almost as much as I breathe. I have worked with amazing collaborators and artists in the last few years who have supported me to clarify my voice, opened up avenues I thought were closed off and created both spaces and platforms for me to develop and share my work. I sincerely thank those who have helped me through life and limitation – my friends, my family, and I would like to acknowledge collaborators Andy Croft, Bob Beagrie, Black Robin and Vici Wreford-Sinnott."

Reach for the Sky

Blood stone canyon
Red sand
Reflecting hot the sun
The sliver of snake skin in the dust,
Survival.

Even the Charity shops have shut.

Lost Chance Saloon

Ash trays churn, turn over,
Flesh hurt, bruised
Noise blotted out in the street,
Life retreats.
Outside in the slammed, shuttered life of the street
The coyote calls of men without work.

Bonanza

The gone shop street
Tries to rally itself one last time.

The old Indian man reaches up to the shelf,
Changing prices on tins of syrup and fruit
With his gun.

He knows they can't compete with the big supermarkets,
Too high the rent, too many bills,
Too much desperation.

Sometimes he is tempted to put a gun to his head.

A splash of blood on the wall,
Next to this week's Bonanza prices.

Marlboro Cowboy

Cowboy man,
Lost in contemplation
Under the brim of his hat,
Galloping through bullet country
Among the slow burning pints,
Ash trays, pork scratchings
And flipped beer mats.

He intends to go out with all guns blazing.

Young Warriors

Narrowed cheekbones, skin lined,
Worn, callous pored,
Wisdom left behind in the dust,
Young warriors,
      The moaning of squaws,
      Lamentation,
      Young warriors,
Lost to the pride of the fight,
The blue-coats,
Homesteads burned,
      Anger arrows,
      War smoke,
Young warriors move to the White Man's city
In search of better things,
The dazzle, the razzle,
The syringe of excitement,
      That left them wanting more,
      Begging on the pavement.

Survivors

In the shadows of rock
The headland of cactus and sand.
Tobacco whiskers,
Spit in the saloon dust.

Red skinned survivors
Of the howling canyon,
They sit in silence like ghosts
So their enemies will not see them.

Outside they listen to
The wind whistling through the high plains,
The coyote call
Of their defeated nation.

Broken Arrow

The white man's promises
Are broken by the silver progress of the railroad.

Cowboys and Indians

The fizz, the surprise,
Punch and Judy, bulls-eyes.

Leapfrog run away, stay,
The dressy up box,
The sawdust circus, the puppet show,
Dandelion and burdock, paper bags,
Pots of gold by the rainbow,
A buttercup under the chin,
He loves me, he loves me not,

Hiding in the bushes,
Childhood ambushes,
The smell of the cap gun,
The crack of the cap,
Childish fun.

Wild West Show

The snake hisses,
The scorpion crawls across the sand,
The crowd applauds.

Children playing cowboys and Indians,
Howling in the yard.

Cactus

Today we are drawing a cactus.

Green fingers spiked,
Pointing to the sky,
Thick crayons,
Drawing a picture of thirst,
The dryness in the throat,
Mickey Mouse ears on the horizon,
Cactus green,
Bulbous spikes,
Dry needles
In a canyon landscape,
Under a cactus sun,
Bad lands.

The sulphur-smell of cap guns.

The Milky Bar Kids

Remember the cat back alley laughter,
Behind the scrub grass fence?
The dirt, the cat scratching,
The purring comic years
Of cross legged fun,
Top Cat, Benny and Officer Dibble,
Quick Draw Mc Graw, *Wiley Cayote*,
Davey Crockett and *The Milky Bar Kid*
With his chocolate and guns?
The pencil thin Indians, the floppy hat,
The draft, the cavalry braid,
Rifles arrows, uniforms?
Men riding rough shod over the plains,
In an alley of metal dustbins and hurt?

Home on the Range

When I was with him I thought I could change,
Live a life of freedom, out on the range,
But Darren was just a local lad.
I waited, sniffed the air.
Smelled something bad.

Fur Trade

Hand smoothes the canoe,
Birch bark shape
Cutting its way through the water,
Birch bark of the fur trade,
Animal rough fur,
Skinned by men in the wilderness,
Dragged down river

To be traded for tobacco, blankets, bear cups,
Broken promises.

Spirit Dance

Geronimo's spirit
Dances in the smoke,
Canyon call of heat and grit,
Circling eagle wings.

Smoking Gun

Tomorrow was the hopes that danced round the totem,
Tomorrow was the breeze stirring the dream catcher,
Ancient whispers, voices held in the feathers,
Chanted stories and ancestral bones
In the depths of the spirit river.

Tomorrow was filled with the White Man's lies.

Rose

Desert rose
The scent of adventure
A glint in the wilderness
The road she chose.

Lonesome

At first I thought someone had made a mistake
When the stage stopped in this godforsaken place.

I stepped out on slender ankles
To be greeted by dust and disorder,

There were men, sprawled in the sand,
Arguing, fighting like animals.

My case was thrown off
Into the unruly, swirling dust.

I'd come to escape, to build a new name
In this expanse of sandiness where you could lose yourself.

What with all the rumours and the false talk
I couldn't go back.

So I swapped my respectable aprons,
And put on these fancy dresses and feathers,

There are no rules here.
You just roll up your sleeves

Pick up your skirt and dance,
Ignore the dirty finger-nails,

The stink of the slag-jawed men
Fumbling with your pretty lace

And use your talents to drain the bottle.
This is a man's world.

Sal's Place

Drooping Damask,
Hanging lace,
Painted face,
Sagging illusions of glamour in Sal's place.

Grandma's Chair

She is growing old,
Her skin is weary,
Her smoothed hair is grey as dust.

She is there in her rocking chair,
Watching the wide plains
For the stage coach
Bringing women, men,
Scarred faces,
Bullets and knives
To her empire of sand.

Bar

I hate that hard bitten chin,
The grit of lip, the lawless grin,
The leather stool he says is his
As he looks at me with that 'kill you' stare.

Enough Rope

The kid who played the gun-slinger,
Horse hoof and stagecoach dust,
Threw his hat in the ring,

Never saw
The tequila dawns,
The whisky sunrises,
And harsh saloons,

The cactus dust,
The masked breath,
The hanging noose.

Breath

Wind twists through the trees,
A wisp of medicine smoke.

Soles of feet palm the earth.

I am dust in the wind,
I am the tremble,
The reverberation,
The light that stirs, touches the flower,
Floating, dangling everywhere,
The dampness of petals.

I am air.

Cold Mountain

Cold land
Harshness's hand
Communicated air smokes
Fists of isolation in the country

Iced sky, unearthed time,
Harvested pumpkin's leer
From furrowed brown fields
Indigo tipped aerials

Rusted signs, lost names
Collieries, factories, cotton works
Farms, lost grass
Gas works, mills, factories, breweries
Teeside, Weardale, Tyneside.

Damp, rust, shorn corn ears
Bending to dirt earth
In furrowed light
Dawn torn horizons

Corn ears sway, twitch,
Damp, rust, harvest dust
Bending to earth,
Furrows of harvest light,
Sour dawn torn horizons.

Feather Dam Adventure

Dreaming days and misspent time,
Hot summer days of catapult and sling shot
Swollen sand banks beneath the viaduct
On the banks of the Wear.

Swirling swish of opalescence,
around the viaduct's feet of stone;
Pearl fins glimmer
The arrow sharp form of the pike.

The kingfisher perches in the trees
Where the branches arch over the river,
Watching for fish in the dam's dark pools,

Where the boy went down,
Swallowed by swirling reeds,
The arrows of death.

Cap Guns and Bandit Scarves

Cowboys and Indians,
Us and Them,
Cap guns and bandit scarves,

Catapults and sling shots,
Scratches and bruises
Spitting on the campfire.

No-one wants to play the baddy,
Wear the black hat,
Be mean, lean
And left for dead.

Lone Ranger

Masked, Gaucho-breathed,
Kemosabe rides alone.
High-ho silver!

Dust flies
As the vulture cries,
Hangs in the skies.

No-one knows his name
Only his bandit eyes.

Always riding to the skyline.

Doc Holliday's Medicine

Doc's health is failing.
The taste is bitter, flaky on the tongue,
These medicines stave away the pain.
He came out west to be a dentist,
But now his TB lungs are fading,
And his face is pale.

Doc rides out,
His life shaded by the brim of his hat.

Bad medicine.

The Darkness of Doc Holliday

He knows they want him gone.
They think he is trouble.
As if he was the cause
Of all the wounds,
The bullet rotting shots,
The distrust, the dust ,
The dirt of the cowhand saloon,.

But a severed limb, now that's a different thing.

Fists, Guns, Dirt

Rage cages the scarred face,
Scuffled roar,
As they scrabble on the floor,
Writhe in sawdust,
Before the wrist, the bullet.

Outside horse manes ripple,
Tied up in the western dirt,
Saddle weary of dipped and purposeful hats,
And lawless men
Before the wrist, the bullet.

Midnight Cowboy

Once he was every girl's fantasy,
A flick of filmic dream,
Blowing in the sand,
Trigger-happy
A never-never bloke,
A wisp of thought
At the end of a hard day's ride.

But life is spiked with thorns and bullets.
Now he limps
Between the Charity shops,
A bullet chipped Old Timer
Trying to survive,
Still ducking and diving
To avoid time's bullets.

Saloon Shutter

Smashed glass shards, glass chin-hurting,
Knuckles suffering, eyes dark and bruised,
He rifles through the rubbish in the alleys,

As the shutters come down.

Garage Gringo

Garage Gringo,
High spaced need of repairs,
Exhaust fume of afternoons,
Jacked up high
On the western ring road,
Petrol pump, dust, grease, oil-gun,
Track, garage, rusted metal,
Petrol gun, oil, ratchet,
Leather cloth, engine,
On the western ring road,
Petrol gun, exhaust dust
Cut and thrust, cut and patch Hatchback.

Carrion characters, searching for scrap
Among the rusted frames and bleached bones.

Compañeros

The two of them were always too young
To be thought of as men,
Boys, youths, fools,
Still roaring at the jokes of childhood,

But when they go out at night
They break into other people's dreams,
Like men, like bandits,

Shaded figures running through back streets,
Bobbing and weaving
Between broken glass and broken promises,

Throwing stones, hanging over the bridge,
Watching the paper boats sail beneath them.

Claim

We are claiming the land,
Those mauve hills,
The pine needle forests,
The spirit rivers,
Taking it back from the red skins.

The hopelessness of the nations.

Hard Work's Wheels

White Man's Truth broken by train-tracks,
Slave labour and broken backs.
Progress.

Before the Flames

Wood planked windows,
Boarded-up doors,
Shuttered shops.
If it's not nailed down
It's yours.

The men are working away.
The women with scooped back hair
Wait for the next attack,
Burning, looting and stealing horses.

The lawless ones come down the chimney.

Hot Western Porch

Hacienda sun,
Baking skin,
Hand shaded eyes.

The sun is blowing dust over the land,
The leather figure looks out,
The horse rears, bullets cut the air.

He sees the rope, hanging.

Blowing in the Wind

Wings circle the sky
Straw scent, horse hooves,
The scarred face, the crooked nose
Saloon whisky breath,
Rye cracked glasses, gambling cards.

The dirt gathered skirt of the saloon leans over to watch.

Cold Landscape

Cold land,
Harsh land,
Freezing air.

Smoke-fists
Of communication.

Tumbleweed

Linoleum marked tables,
Coffee mugs.
I warm my hands
To hold off the distress
That marks this town.

Line Dance

Everyone else is wearing leathers and hats,
Tassels and western boots
As they move in out,
In and out, in and out.
Take your partner by the arm, swing him round,
You don't want to be here,

Heels click, obeying the tannoy voice,
In their jagged jazzy checked outfits
In and out, in and out,
In and out, in and out.
Take your partner by the arm, swing him round,

You cringe away from the music, the instructions,
As usual you shrink to the shadows.

Time to saddle up and go, you reckon.

Bottle

Sasparilla sunset,
Where the sky meets the dry earth,
And the cowboys face the Indians.

Pistol point hatred,
Pale faces and unbelonging faces.

Tar on the flesh,
Cigarettes,
Drunken arguments,
Shadow wanderings,
The threats of men
Who stare at the sky in despair.

Gone West

'Go West,' my friend said.
Alright for him,
He was a rebel.
Principles, politics,
He said he had both.
'Go West,' he said.

He said he believed in peace,
But he said nothing when they sent in the cavalry
And the striking miners were taken away, truncheoned, put in
cells.

He said he believed in the future,
But he said nothing when they served poverty on a plate to the
people,
Beating those who resisted.

Soldier Blue

Of course there were a few who regretted their actions that day,
The plumes of smoke,
The burning skin of the teepees,
The burning skin of the children
In the wigwam bruised air;

The last of the Great Chiefs was brought in,
Caged, whispered over,
Humbled and humiliated
His nation forced to kneel in burnt earth and poverty;

The promises,
The deceit,
Feathers lost to the horizon,
Where the water meets the sky.

Ashes

Charcoal life,
Art, blood plant dyes,
Stitches sewed by women
Kneeling round the fire.

Charcoal life.
The cavalry,
The law,
Burning everything in their path.

Under Western Skies

Eagles fly and vultures cry,
The law is a coin in the dust with two faces,
Beaten brims and Indian skins,
Spurs jangle, under the harsh sun,
Sheriff's badge, snake bite saloon,
Broken bank, crag hurt,
Boot hill gravestones,
Where the famous dead are left alone.

Enough

Enough.
This life of fag ash, dust
And distrust.

Till Then

Tomorrow comes
Drifting down
Over the cactus horizon.

Sundown

Night of noise and raucousness
Drunken nights of darkness kicking life,
Cold evenings of dust and moonshine.

Footfall

Step back this time from the fenced in feeling,
The piercing wolf howls
Of those who have lost everything.

Desert

There is music in the desert:

The howl, the call,
The dry echo,
The soaring cry,
The hidden claws,
The mountain paws
The moaning chants of desolation.

Bar Room Cowboy

He holds the reins tight and sits on the saddle
Of a bucking bronco machine
In a bar in Crook, Co. Durham.
Ride 'em cowboy!

It's his fortieth birthday
And he is wearing the face
Of a man with a skin full of beer.

As usual, a man speaking out of his rear,
Saying things he won't remember in the morning,

He tries to hold on.

One Armed Bandits

The wooden floor of the bar,
Draught from the door,
Spitting rage,
The malice flick of peanuts,
As bored men slump over their drinks.

Tequila life, hidden
Behind slot-machines,
Betting-machines,
Music machines.

Life coughs up the remnants.

Old Timer

He lags behind the rest
A limp-along cowboy,
Once a miner,
He now counts out his future in coins from a jar,
As he takes his seat at the end of the bar.

He calculates every penny, holds tight to every pound,
His meager pension must go round and round.

Outlaw

Graffiti dribbles down the wall,
Bleeding red letters, the names of men.

The Outlaw comes out of the shadows,
Between the mist of cactus dust,
And the horse's whinny,

His balaclava pulled down,
The Outlaw is on the town.

Tired Night

Shop receipts, carrier bags,
Fat women, slags,
But all I want tonight,
Is a companion,
A table cloth,
Popadoms, cinnamon,
Popadoms, cardamom.

An Indian.

Me & Hiawatha

Drifting down the chanting river
To the shores of Gitchee Gumee,

He called me his laughing water,
Said I was graceful as a birch canoe, bark-skinned, narrow.

He moved through the tall trees
With his cloak and knife.

Silent Running Silver Water,
Under a moon of leaves,

Bow and cord,
Heart and hand.

Now shadows sift the water reeds
Around the empty moon.

Minnehaha & Me

By the singing river, silver ripples,
The memory of Minnehaha bends

In the waterfalls' rippling patterns
In the weave of patterned blankets,
In the dreaming circle,
On the silver horizon
Suppressing the rustle of fright.

I thought he would stay and fight.

Run Free

Red rock dust,
The echo of a wild horse
Galloping through the canyon,
Mane flowing in the breeze.

My life is running away from me.

Cornershop Cowgirl

The whole world spins against me,
As I choose the point of the compass
That will help me best:
North, South, East or West.

IRON Press is among the country's longest
established independent literary publishers. The
press began operations in 1973 with IRON Magazine
which ran for 83 editions until 1997. Since 1975 we
have also brought out a regular list of individual
collections of poetry, fiction and drama plus various
anthologies ranging from *The Poetry of Perestroika*,
through *Limerick Nation* and *Cold IRON - 21st
Century Ghost Stories*.

We are also one of the leading independent
publishers of haiku in the UK.
Since 2013 we have also run a regular IRON Press
Festival round the harbourfront in our native
Cullercoats.We are delighted to be a part of Inpress
Ltd, which was set up by Arts Council England to
support independent literary publishers.
Go to our website (www.ironpress.co.uk)
for full details of our titles and activities.

Lightning Source UK Ltd.
Milton Keynes UK
UKOW03f0312110317

296352UK00002B/71/P